The Illustrated Book
of Children's Verse

Publisher and Creative Director: Nick Wells
Project Editor and Picture Research: Emma Chafer
and Esme Chapman
Special thanks to Laura Bulbeck and Catherine Taylor

This edition first published 2014 by
FLAME TREE PUBLISHING
Crabtree Hall, Crabtree Lane
Fulham, London SW6 6TY
United Kingdom

www.flametreepublishing.com

14 16 18 17 15
1 3 5 7 9 10 8 6 4 2

© 2014 Flame Tree Publishing Ltd

ISBN 978-1-78361-130-0

A CIP record for this book is available from the British Library
upon request.

Every effort has been made to contact copyright holders. In the event
of an oversight the publishers would be glad to rectify any omissions
in future editions of this book.

Printed in China

The Illustrated Book
of Children's Verse

A special selection edited by
E. I. Chafer & E. A. Chapman

FLAME TREE
PUBLISHING

Contents

Introduction

here is no greater joy than sharing a wonderful poem with a child, seeing their face light up with imagination and hearing delight when they recite their favourite verse by heart. From the very first nursery rhymes shared with babies to the more demanding narrative poems of adolescence – children really do enjoy being entertained by the poetic word. By encouraging them to explore their imagination through poetry, children improve their literacy and vocabulary skills as well as appreciating that the simplest things in the world can be poetic too. Edward Lear (1812-88) – among others – has captured the attention of children for years and is sure to continue for years to come with his delightful poem *The Owl and The Pussy-Cat*. Rich in alliteration and repetition and interwoven with a charming animal narrative, it is a poem both children and adults alike can enjoy.

Beginning with a section of 'Fable Poems', these verses highlight how poems encompassed with a moral are still popular and meaningful to children, even today. This anthology brings together the work of nineteenth – and early twentieth – century British poets from Alfred, Lord Tennyson (1809-92) and Rudyard Kipling (1865–1936) to the works of American novelist and poet Louisa May Alcott (1832-88). Edward Lear also makes a substantial contribution to this

collection with his ever-popular nonsense poems. *The Quangle Wangle's Hat* is a humorous and highly nonsensical poem drawing moral wisdom from the happiness that friendship can bring.

Despite the important messages that fable poems can translate to children, there is a wide range of other thematic verse that can impart the diversity of language. Animals play a huge part in many children's lives, whether keeping kittens as pets, taking a walk in the countryside amongst the many cows, sheep and horses that inhabit the green pastures or even encountering exotic species in a zoo. With contributions from William Blake (1757-1827) and Samuel Taylor Coleridge (1772-1834) the section 'Animal Poems' offers choices suitable for every type of animal lover.

Much poetic verse with its gentle rhythms and repetitive nature make bedtime for children – and adults – a more pleasant experience. Whether it is a lullaby designed to encourage young ones to succumb to a peaceful slumber, or a comforting prayer, the section of 'Bedtime Poems' will offer words of comfort at a sometimes-stressful time.

Through a chapter of poems dedicated to the 'Natural World', this anthology concludes by exploring how children find the wonder of nature in the world around them. From the very first instance of being able to speak, children begin to question the world in which they live. Whether it is a trip to the seaside, bucket and spade in hand, or the first frost of winter sparkling like glitter, they seek out answers about nature, satisfying their curiosity only with another question. Famous for expressing her definition of natural beauty Christina Rossetti's (1830-94) *The Rainbow* is a firm reminder that – even though manmade structures can be alluring – there is often nothing more beautiful than nature itself.

Exploring varied themes, this collection portrays poetry that will be shared by children and adults alike in an attempt to enjoy the diverse selection of language, narrative and rhythm found in children's verse.

Fable Poems

The Little Doll
Charles Kingsley (1819–75)

I once had a sweet little doll, dears,
The prettiest doll in the world;
Her cheeks were so red and so white; dears,
And her hair was so charmingly curled.

But I lost my poor little doll, dears,
As I played in the heath one day;
And I cried for her more than a week, dears;
But I never could find where she lay.

I found my poor little doll, dears,
As I played in the heath one day:
Folks say she is terrible changed, dears,
For her paint is all washed away,
And her arm trodden off by the cows, dears,
And her hair not the least bit curled:
Yet for old sakes' sake she is still, dears,
The prettiest doll in the world.

Sweet and Low
Alfred, Lord Tennyson (1809–92)

Sweet and low, sweet and low,
Wind of the western sea,
Low, low, breathe and blow,
Wind of the western sea!
Over the rolling waters go,
Come from the dying moon and blow,
Blow him again to me;
While my little one, while my pretty one sleeps.

Sleep and rest, sleep and rest,
Father will come to thee soon;
Rest, rest, on mother's breast,
Father will come to thee soon;
Father will come to his babe in the nest,
Silver sails all out of the west
Under the silver moon:
Sleep, my little one, sleep, my pretty one, sleep.

Suppose
Phoebe Cary (1824–71)

Suppose, my little lady,
Your doll should break her head,
Could you make it whole by crying
Till your eyes and nose are red?
And wouldn't it be pleasanter
To treat it as a joke;
And say you're glad "'T was Dolly's
And not your head that broke?"

Suppose you're dressed for walking,
And the rain comes pouring down,
Will it clear off any sooner
Because you scold and frown?
And wouldn't it be nicer
For you to smile than pout,
And so make sunshine in the house
When there is none without?

Suppose your task, my little man,
Is very hard to get,
Will it make it any easier
For you to sit and fret?
And wouldn't it be wiser

Than waiting like a dunce,
To go to work in earnest
And learn the thing at once?

Suppose that some boys have a horse,
And some a coach and pair,
Will it tire you less while walking
To say, "It isn't fair?"
And wouldn't it be nobler
To keep your temper sweet,
And in your heart be thankful
You can walk upon your feet?

And suppose the world don't please you,
Nor the way some people do,
Do you think the whole creation
Will be altered just for you?
And isn't it, my boy or girl,
The wisest, bravest plan,
Whatever comes, or doesn't come,
To do the best you can?

Don't Give Up
Phoebe Cary (1824–71)

If you've tried and have not won,
Never stop for trying;
All that's good and great is done
Just by patient trying.

Though young birds, in flying, fall,
Still their wings grow stronger,
And the next time they can keep
Up a little longer.

Though the sturdy oak has known
Many a wind that bowed her,
She has risen again and grown
Loftier and prouder.

If by easy work you beat,
Who the more will prize you?
Gaining victory from defeat,
That's the test that tries you.

The Story of Johnny Head-in-the-Air (extract)

Heinrich Hoffman (1809–94)

As he trudged along to school,
It was always Johnny's rule
To be looking at the sky
And the clouds that floated by;
But what just before him lay,
In his way,
Johnny never thought about;
So that everyone cried out,
"Look at little Johnny there,
Little Johnny Head-in-Air!"

Running just in Johnny's way
Came a little dog one day;
Johnny's eyes were still astray
Up on high,
In the sky;
And he never heard them cry
"Johnny, mind, the dog is nigh!"
Bump!
Dump!
Down they fell, with such a thump,
Dog and Johnny in a lump!

Once, with head as high as ever,
Johnny walked beside the river.
Johnny watched the swallows trying
Which was cleverest at flying.
Oh! What fun!
Johnny watched the bright round sun
Going in and coming out;
This was all he thought about.
So he strode on, only think!
To the river's very brink,
Where the bank was and steep,
And the water very deep;
And the fishes, in a row,
Stared to see him coming so.

One step more! oh! sad to tell!
Headlong in poor Johnny fell.
And the fishes, in dismay,
Wagged their tails and swam away.

Bob White
George Cooper (c. 1838–1927)

I see you, on the zigzag rails,
You cheery little fellow!
While purple leaves are whirling down,
And scarlet, brown, and yellow.
I hear you when the air is full
Of snow-down of the thistle;
All in your speckled jacket trim,
"Bob White! Bob White!" you whistle.

Tall amber sheaves, in rustling rows,
Are nodding there to greet you;
I know that you are out for play–
How I should like to meet you!
Though blithe of voice, so shy you are,
In this delightful weather;
What splendid playmates you and I,
"Bob White," would make together!

There, you are gone! but far away
I hear your whistle falling.
Ah! may be it is hide-and-seek,
And that's why you are calling.
Along those hazy uplands wide
We'd be such merry rangers;
What! silent now, and hidden too?
"Bob White," don't let's be strangers.

Perhaps you teach your brood the game,
In yonder rainbowed thicket,
While winds are playing with the leaves,
And softly creaks the cricket.
"Bob White! Bob White!"– again I hear
That blithely whistled chorus;
Why should we not companions be?
One Father watches o'er us!

Little Boy Blue

Eugene Field (1850–95)

The little toy dog is covered with dust,
But sturdy and stanch he stands;
And the little toy soldier is red with rust,
And his musket moulds in his hands.
Time was when the little toy dog was new,
And the soldier was passing fair;
And that was the time when our Little Boy Blue
Kissed them and put them there.

"Now, don't you go till I come," he said,
"And don't you make any noise!"
So, toddling off to his trundle-bed,
He dreamt of the pretty toys;
And, as he was dreaming, an angel song
Awakened our Little Boy Blue –
Oh! the years are many, the years are long,
But the little toy friends are true!

Ay, faithful to Little Boy Blue they stand,
Each in the same old place –
Awaiting the touch of a little hand,
The smile of a little face;
And they wonder, as waiting the long years through
In the dust of that little chair,
What has become of our Little Boy Blue,
Since he kissed them and put them there.

The Story of Fidgety Philip
Heinrich Hoffman (1809–94)

"Let me see if Philip can
Be a little gentleman;
Let me see if he is able
To sit still for once at table:"
Thus Papa bade Phil behave;
And Mamma looked very grave.
But fidgety Phil,
He won't sit still;
He wriggles,
And giggles,
And then, I declare,
Swings backwards and forwards,
And tilts up his chair,
Just like any rocking-horse –
"Philip! I am getting cross!"

See the naughty, restless child
Growing still more rude and wild,
Till his chair falls over quite.
Philip screams with all his might,
Catches at the cloth, but then
That makes matters worse again.

Down upon the ground they fall,
Glasses, plates, knives, forks, and all.
How Mamma did fret and frown,
When she saw them tumbling down!
And Papa made such a face!
Philip is in sad disgrace.

Where is Philip, where is he?
Fairly covered up you see!
Cloth and all are lying on him;
He has pulled down all upon him.
What a terrible to-do!
Dishes, glasses, snapped in two!
Here a knife, and there a fork!
Philip, this is cruel work.
Table all so bare, and ah!
Poor Papa, and poor Mamma
Look quite cross, and wonder how
They shall have their dinner now.

A Fairy Tale
Helen Gray Cone (1859–1934)

There stands by the wood-path shaded
 A meek little beggar maid;
Close under her mantle faded
 She is hidden like one afraid.

Yet if you but lifted lightly
 That mantle of russet brown,
She would spring up slender and sightly,
 In a smoke-blue silken gown.

For she is a princess, fated,
 Disguised in the wood to dwell,
And all her life long has awaited
 The touch that should break the spell;

And the Oak, that has cast around her
 His root like a wrinkled arm,
Is the wild old wizard that bound her
 Fast with his cruel charm.

Is the princess worth your knowing?
 Then haste, for the spring is brief,
And find the Hepatica growing,
 Hid under a last year's leaf!

There Was a Little Girl
Henry Wadsworth Longfellow (1807–82)

There was a little girl
Who had a little curl
Right in the middle of her forehead.
When she was good
She was very good indeed,
But when she was bad she was horrid.

Topsy Turvey World (extract)
William Brighty Rands (1823–82)

If the butterfly courted the bee,
And the owl the porcupine;
If the churches were built in the sea,
And three times one was nine;
If the pony rode his master,
If the buttercups ate the cows,
If the cat had the dire disaster
To be worried, sir, by the mouse;
If mamma, sir, sold the baby
To a gypsy for half-a-crown;
If a gentleman, sir, was a lady –
The world would be Upside Down!
If any or all of these wonders
Should ever come about,
I should not consider them blunders,
For I should be Inside Out!

If—
Rudyard Kipling (1865–1936)

If you can keep your head when all about you
    Are losing theirs and blaming it on you,
If you can trust yourself when all men doubt you,
    But make allowance for their doubting too;
If you can wait and not be tired by waiting,
    Or being lied about, don't deal in lies,
Or being hated, don't give way to hating,
    And yet don't look too good, nor talk too wise:

If you can dream—and not make dreams your master;
    If you can think—and not make thoughts your aim;
If you can meet with Triumph and Disaster
    And treat those two impostors just the same;
If you can bear to hear the truth you've spoken
    Twisted by knaves to make a trap for fools,
Or watch the things you gave your life to, broken,
    And stoop and build 'em up with worn-out tools:

If you can make one heap of all your winnings
    And risk it on one turn of pitch-and-toss,
And lose, and start again at your beginnings
    And never breathe a word about your loss;
If you can force your heart and nerve and sinew
    To serve your turn long after they are gone,

And so hold on when there is nothing in you
   Except the will which says to them: 'Hold on!'

If you can talk with crowds and keep your virtue,
   Or walk with Kings—nor lose the common touch,
If neither foes nor loving friends can hurt you,
   If all men count with you, but none too much;
If you can fill the unforgiving minute
   With sixty seconds' worth of distance run,
Yours is the Earth and everything that's in it,
   And – which is more – you'll be a Man, my son!

A Song from the Suds
Louisa May Alcott (1832–88)

Queen of my tub, I merrily sing,
While the white foam raises high,
And sturdily wash, and rinse, and wring,
And fasten the clothes to dry;
Then out in the free fresh air they swing,
Under the sunny sky.

I wish we could wash from our hearts and our souls
The stains of the week away,
And let water and air by their magic make
Ourselves as pure as they;
Then on the earth there would be indeed
A glorious washing day!

Along the path of a useful life
Will heart's-ease ever bloom;
The busy mind has no time to think
Of sorrow, or care, or gloom;
And anxious thoughts may be swept away
As we busily wield a broom.

I am glad a task to me is given
To labor at day by day;
For it brings me health, and strength, and hope,
And I cheerfully learn to say –
"Head, you may think; heart, you may feel;
But hand, you shall work always!"

The Quangle Wangle's Hat (extract)
Edward Lear (1812–88)

On the top of the Crumpetty Tree
    The Quangle Wangle sat,
But his face you could not see,
    On account of his Beaver Hat.
For his Hat was a hundred and two feet wide,
With ribbons and bibbons on every side
And bells, and buttons, and loops, and lace,
So that nobody ever could see the face
      Of the Quangle Wangle Quee.

The Quangle Wangle said
    To himself on the Crumpetty Tree, –
"Jam; and jelly; and bread;
    Are the best of food for me!
But the longer I live on this Crumpetty Tree
The plainer than ever it seems to me
That very few people come this way
And that life on the whole is far from gay!"
      Said the Quangle Wangle Quee.

But there came to the Crumpetty Tree,
    Mr. and Mrs. Canary;
And they said, – "Did ever you see
    Any spot so charmingly airy?
May we build a nest on your lovely Hat?

Mr. Quangle Wangle, grant us that!
O please let us come and build a nest
Of whatever material suits you best,
    Mr. Quangle Wangle Quee!"

And besides, to the Crumpetty Tree
    Came the Stork, the Duck, and the Owl;
The Snail, and the Bumble-Bee,
    The Frog, and the Fimble Fowl;
(The Fimble Fowl, with a corkscrew leg;)
And all of them said, – "We humbly beg,
We may build out homes on your lovely Hat, –
Mr. Quangle Wangle, grant us that!
    Mr. Quangle Wangle Quee!"

And the Golden Grouse came there,
    And the Pobble who has no toes, –
And the small Olympian bear, –
    And the Dong with a luminous nose.
And the Blue Baboon, who played the Flute, –
And the Orient Calf from the Land of Tute, –
And the Attery Squash, and the Bisky Bat, –
All came and built on the lovely Hat
    Of the Quangle Wangle Quee.

Animal Poems

The Tyger
(from Songs Of Experience)
William Blake (1757 – 1827)

Tyger! Tyger! burning bright
In the forests of the night,
What immortal hand or eye
Could frame thy fearful symmetry?

In what distant deeps or skies
Burnt the fire of thine eyes?
On what wings dare he aspire?
What the hand dare seize the fire?

And what shoulder, and what art.
Could twist the sinews of thy heart?
And when thy heart began to beat,
What dread hand? and what dread feet?

What the hammer? what the chain?
In what furnace was thy brain?
What the anvil? what dread grasp
Dare its deadly terrors clasp?

When the stars threw down their spears,
And watered heaven with their tears,
Did he smile his work to see?
Did he who made the Lamb make thee?

Tyger! Tyger! burning bright
In the forests of the night,
What immortal hand or eye
Dare frame thy fearful symmetry?

The Lobster Quadrille
Lewis Carroll (1832–98)

"Will you walk a little faster?" said a whiting to a snail.
"There's a porpoise close behind us, and he's treading on my tail.
See how eagerly the lobsters and the turtles all advance!
They are waiting on the shingle - will you come and join the dance?
Will you, won't you, will you, won't you, will you join the dance?
Will you, won't you, will you, won't you, won't you join the dance?

"You can really have no notion how delightful it will be
When they take us up and throw us, with the lobsters, out to sea!"
But the snail replied "Too far, too far!" and gave a look askance –
Said he thanked the whiting kindly, but he would not join the dance.
Would not, could not, would not, could not, would not join the dance.
Would not, could not, would not, could not, could not join the dance.

"What matters it how far we go?" his scaly friend replied.
"There is another shore, you know, upon the other side.
The further off from England the nearer is to France –
Then turn not pale, beloved snail, but come and join the dance.
Will you, won't you, will you, won't you, will you join the dance?
Will you, won't you, will you, won't you, won't you join the dance?"

The Duck and the Kangaroo
Edward Lear (1812–88)

Said the Duck to the Kangaroo,
'Good gracious! how you hop!
Over the fields and the water too,
As if you never would stop!
My life is a bore in this nasty pond,
And I long to go out in the world beyond!
I wish I could hop like you!'
Said the Duck to the Kangaroo.

'Please give me a ride on your back!'
Said the Duck to the Kangaroo.
'I would sit quite still, and say nothing but 'Quack',
The whole of the long day through!
And we'd go to the Dee, and the Jelly Bo Lee,
Over the land, and over the sea;
Please take me a ride! O do!'
Said the Duck to the Kangaroo.

Said the Kangaroo to the Duck,
'This requires some little reflection;
Perhaps on the whole it might bring me luck,
And there seems but one objection,
Which is, if you'll let me speak so bold,
Your feet are unpleasantly wet and cold,
And would probably give me the roo-
Matiz!' said the Kangaroo.

Said the Duck, 'As I sat on the rocks,
I have thought over that completely,
And I bought four pairs of worsted socks
Which fit my web-feet neatly.
And to keep out the cold I've bought a cloak,
And every day a cigar I'll smoke,
All to follow my own dear true
Love of a Kangaroo!'

Said the Kangaroo, 'I'm ready!
'All in the moonlight pale;
'But to balance me well, dear Duck, sit steady!
'And quite at the end of my tail!'
So away they went with a hop and a bound,
And they hopped the whole world three times round;
And who so happy – O who,
As the Duck and the Kangaroo?

The Owl
Alfred, Lord Tennyson (1809–92)

When cats run home and light is come,
And dew is cold upon the ground,
And the far-off stream is dumb,
And the whirring sail goes round,
And the whirring sail goes round;
Alone and warming his five wits,
The white owl in the belfry sits.

When merry milkmaids click the latch,
And rarely smells the new-mown hay,
And the cock hath sung beneath the thatch
Twice or thrice his roundelay,
Twice or thrice his roundelay;
Alone and warming his five wits,
The white owl in the belfry sits.

The Lamb
William Blake (1757 – 1827)

Little lamb, who made thee?
Dost thou know who made thee?
Gave thee life, and bid thee feed
By the stream and o'er the mead;
Gave thee clothing of delight,
Softest clothing, woolly, bright;
Gave thee such a tender voice,
Making all the vales rejoice?
Little lamb, who made thee?
Dost thou know who made thee?

Little lamb, I'll tell thee,
Little lamb, I'll tell thee:
He is called by thy name,
For He calls Himself a lamb.
He is meek, and He is mild;
He became a little child.
I a child, and thou a lamb,
We are called by His name.
Little lamb, God bless thee!
Little lamb, God bless thee!

At The Zoo
William Makepeace Thackeray (1811–63)

First I saw the white bear, then I saw the black;

Then I saw the camel with a hump upon his back;

Then I saw the grey wolf, with mutton in his maw;

Then I saw the wombat waddle in the straw;

Then I saw the elephant a-waving of his trunk;

Then I saw the monkeys – mercy, how unpleasantly they smelt!

The Fieldmouse
Cecil Frances Alexander (1818–95)

Where the acorn tumbles down,
Where the ash tree sheds its berry,
With your fur so soft and brown,
With your eye so round and merry,
Scarcely moving the long grass,
Fieldmouse, I can see you pass.

Little thing, in what dark den,
Lie you all the winter sleeping?
Till warm weather comes again,
Then once more I see you peeping
Round about the tall tree roots,
Nibbling at their fallen fruits.

Fieldmouse, fieldmouse, do not go,
Where the farmer stacks his treasure,
Find the nut that falls below,
Eat the acorn at your pleasure,
But you must not steal the grain
He has stacked with so much pain.

Make your hole where mosses spring,
Underneath the tall oak's shadow,
Pretty, quiet harmless thing,
Play about the sunny meadow.
Keep away from corn and house,
None will harm you, little mouse.

The Cow
Robert Louis Stevenson (1850–94)

The friendly cow, all red and white,
I love with all my heart:
She gives me cream with all her might,
To eat with apple tart.

She wanders lowing here and there,
And yet she cannot stray,
All in the pleasant open air,
The pleasant light of day;

And blown by all the winds that pass
And wet with all the showers,
She walks among the meadow grass
And eats the meadow flowers.

Fraidie-Cat
Clinton Scollard (1860 – 1932)

I shan't tell you what's his name:
When we want to play a game,
Always thinks that he'll be hurt,
Soil his jacket in the dirt,
Tear his trousers, spoil his hat, –
Fraidie-Cat! Fraidie-Cat!

Nothing of the boy in him!
"Dasn't" try to learn to swim;
Says a cow'll hook; if she
Looks at him he'll climb a tree;
"Scart" to death at bee or bat, –
Fraidie-Cat! Fraidie-Cat!

Claims there're ghosts all snowy white
Wandering around at night
In the attic; wouldn't go
There for anything, I know;
B'lieve he'd run if you said "Scat!"
Fraidie-Cat! Fraidie-Cat!

The Camel's Hump
Rudyard Kipling (1865–1936)

The Camel's hump is an ugly lump
Which well you may see at the Zoo;
But uglier yet is the hump we get
From having too little to do.

Kiddies and grown-ups too-oo-oo,
If we haven't enough to do-oo-oo,
We get the hump –
Cameelious hump –
The hump that is black and blue!

We climb out of bed with a frouzly head,
And a snarly-yarly voice.
We shiver and scowl and we grunt and we growl
At our bath and our boots and our toys;

And there ought to be a corner for me
(And I know there is one for you)
When we get the hump –
Cameelious hump –
The hump that is black and blue!

The cure for this ill is not to sit still,
Or frowst with a book by the fire;
But to take a large hoe and a shovel also,
And dig till you gently perspire;

And then you will find that the sun and the wind,
And the Djinn of the Garden too,
Have lifted the hump –
The horrible hump –
The hum that is black and blue!

I get it as well as you-oo-oo –
If I haven't enough to do-oo-oo!
We all get hump –
Cameelious hump –
Kiddies and grown-ups too!

The Ostrich
Mary E. Wilkins Freeman (1852–1930)

The ostrich is a silly bird,
  With scarcely any mind.
He often runs so very fast,
  He leaves himself behind.

And when he gets there, has to stand
  And hang about till night,
Without a blessed thing to do
  Until he comes in sight.

Eletelephony
Laura Richards (1850–1943)

Once there was an elephant,
Who tried to use the telephant –
No! No! I mean an elephone
Who tried to use the telephone –
(Dear me! I am not certain quite
That even now I've got it right.)

Howe'er it was, he got his trunk
Entangled in the telephunk;
The more he tried to get it free,
The louder buzzed the telephee –
(I fear I'd better drop the song
Of elephop and telephong!)

Two Little Kittens
Anonymous (c. 1880)

Two little kittens, one stormy night,
Began to quarrel, and then to fight;
One had a mouse, the other had none,
And that's the way the quarrel begun.

"I'll have that mouse," said the biggest cat;
"You'll have that mouse? We'll see about that!"
"I will have that mouse," said the eldest son;
"You shan't have the mouse," said the little one.

I told you before 'twas a stormy night
When these two little kittens began to fight;
The old woman seized her sweeping broom,
And swept the two kittens right out of the room.

The ground was covered with frost and snow,
And the two little kittens had nowhere to go;
So they laid them down on the mat at the door,
While the old woman finished sweeping the floor.

Then they crept in, as quiet as mice,
All wet with the snow, and cold as ice,
For they found it was better, that stormy night,
To lie down and sleep than to quarrel and fight.

If I Had But Two Little Wings
Samuel Taylor Coleridge (1772–1834)

If I had but two little wings
And were a little feathery bird,
To you I'd fly, my dear!
But thoughts like these are idle things
And I stay here.

But in my sleep to you I fly:
I'm always with you in my sleep!
The world is all one's own.
And then one wakes, and where am I?
All, all alone.

The Owl and the Pussy-Cat

Edward Lear (1812–88)

The Owl and the Pussy-cat went to sea
　In a beautiful pea-green boat,
They took some honey, and plenty of money,
　Wrapped up in a five-pound note.
The Owl looked up to the stars above,
　And sang to a small guitar,
"O lovely Pussy! O Pussy, my love,
　What a beautiful Pussy you are,
　　　You are,
　　　You are!
What a beautiful Pussy you are!"

Pussy said to the Owl, "You elegant fowl!
　How charmingly sweet you sing!
O let us be married! too long we have tarried:
　But what shall we do for a ring?"
They sailed away, for a year and a day,
　To the land where the Bong-Tree grows
And there in a wood a Piggy-wig stood
　With a ring at the end of his nose,
　　　His nose,
　　　His nose,
With a ring at the end of his nose.

"Dear Pig, are you willing to sell for one shilling
  Your ring?" Said the Piggy, "I will."
So they took it away, and were married next day
  By the Turkey who lives on the hill.
They dined on mince, and slices of quince,
  Which they ate with a runcible spoon;
And hand in hand, on the edge of the sand,
  They danced by the light of the moon,
      The moon,
      The moon,
They danced by the light of the moon.

Jabberwocky
Lewis Carroll (1832–98)

'Twas brillig, and the slithy toves
Did gyre and gimble in the wabe:
All mimsy were the borogoves,
And the mome raths outgrabe.

"Beware the Jabberwock, my son!
The jaws that bite, the claws that catch!
Beware the Jubjub bird, and shun
The frumious Bandersnatch!"

He took his vorpal sword in hand:
Long time the manxome foe he sought
So rested he by the Tumtum tree,
And stood a while in thought.

And, as in uffish thought he stood,
The Jabberwock, with eyes of flame,
Came whiffling through the tulgey wood,
And burbled as it came!

One two! One two! And through and through
The vorpal blade went snicker-snack!
He left it dead, and with its head
He went galumphing back.

"And hast thou slain the Jabberwock?
Come to my arms, my beamish boy!
Oh frabjous day! Callooh! Callay!"
He chortled in his joy.

'Twas brillig, and the slithy toves
Did gyre and gimble in the wabe:
All mimsy were the borogoves,
And the mome raths outgrabe.

A Guinea Pig
Anonymous (c. 1775)

There was a little guinea pig,
Who being little, was not big;
He always walked upon his feet,
And never fasted when he eat.

When from a place he run away,
He never at the place did stay;
And while he run, as I am told,
He never stood still for young or old.

He often squeaked, and sometimes violent,
And when he squeaked he never was silent.
Though never instructed by a cat,
He knew a mouse was not a rat.

One day, as I am certified,
He took a whim, and fairly died;
And as I am told by men of sense,
He never has been living since.

Mary's Lamb
Sarah Josepha Hale (1788–1879)

Mary had a little lamb,
Its fleece was white as snow,
And everywhere that Mary went
The lamb was sure to go;
He followed her to school one day –
That was against the rule,
It made the children laugh and play
To see a lamb at school.

And so the teacher turned him out,
But still he lingered near,
And waited patiently about,
Till Mary did appear.
And then he ran to her and laid
His head upon her arm,
As if he said, "I'm not afraid –
You'll shield me from all harm."

"What makes the lamb love Mary so?"
The little children cry;
"Oh, Mary loves the lamb, you know,"
The teacher did reply,
"And, you, each gentle animal
In confidence may bind,
And make it follow at your call,
If you are always kind."

Bedtime Poems

Cradle Song
William Blake (1757–1827)

Sleep, sleep, beauty bright,
Dreaming in the joys of night;
Sleep, sleep; in thy sleep
Little sorrows sit and weep.

Sweet babe, in thy face
Soft desires I can trace,
Secret joys and secret smiles,
Little pretty infant wiles.

As thy softest limbs I feel
Smiles as of the morning steal
O'er thy cheek, and o'er thy breast
Where thy little heart doth rest.

O the cunning wiles that creep
In thy little heart asleep!
When thy little heart doth wake,
Then the dreadful night shall break.

Japanese Lullaby
Eugene Field (1850–95)

Sleep, little pigeon, and fold your wings, –
Little blue pigeon with velvet eyes;
Sleep to the singing of mother-bird swinging –
Swinging the nest where her little one lies.

Away out yonder I see a star, –
Silvery star with a tinkling song;
To the soft dew falling I hear it calling –
Calling and tinkling the night along.

In through the window a moonbeam comes, –
Little gold moonbeam with misty wings;
All silently creeping, it asks, "Is he sleeping –
Sleeping and dreaming while mother sings?"

Up from the sea there floats the sob
Of the waves that are breaking upon the shore,
As though they were groaning in anguish, and moaning –
Bemoaning the ship that shall come no more.

But sleep, little pigeon, and fold your wings, –
Little blue pigeon with mournful eyes;
Am I not singing? – see, I am swinging –
Swinging the nest where my darling lies.

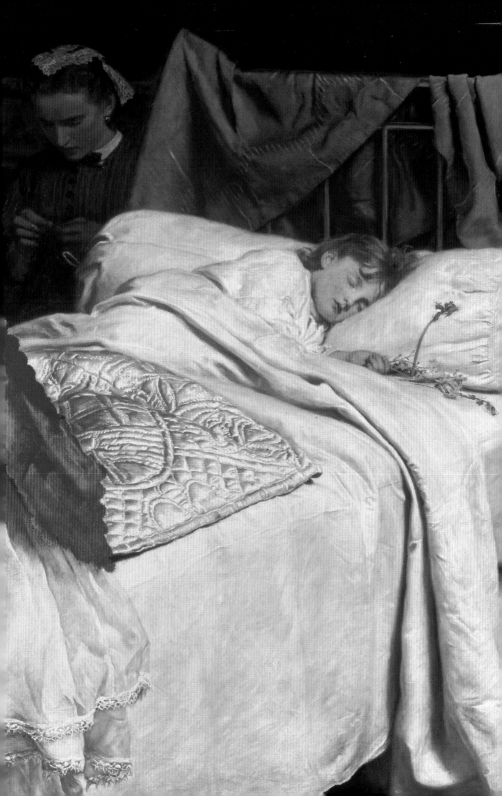

The Sugar-Plum Tree
Eugene Field (1850–95)

Have you ever heard of the Sugar-Plum Tree?
'Tis a marvel of great renown!
It blooms on the shore of the Lollypop sea
In the garden of Shut-Eye Town;
The fruit that it bears is so wondrously sweet
(As those who have tasted it say)
That good little children have only to eat
Of that fruit to be happy next day.

When you've got to the tree, you would have a hard time
To capture the fruit which I sing;
The tree is so tall that no person could climb
To the boughs where the sugar-plums swing!
But up in that tree sits a chocolate cat,
And a gingerbread dog prowls below –
And this is the way you contrive to get at
Those sugar-plums tempting you so:

You say but the word to that gingerbread dog
And he barks with such terrible zest
That the chocolate cat is at once all agog,
As her swelling proportions attest.
And the chocolate cat goes cavorting around
From this leafy limb unto that,
And the sugar-plums tumble, of course, to the ground –
Hurrah for that chocolate cat!

There are marshmallows, gumdrops, and peppermint canes,

With stripings of scarlet or gold,

And you carry away of the treasure that rains,

As much as your apron can hold!

So come, little child, cuddle closer to me

In your dainty white nightcap and gown,

And I'll rock you away to that Sugar-Plum Tree

In the garden of Shut-Eye Town.

A Boat, Beneath a Sunny Sky

Lewis Carroll (1832–98)

A boat, beneath a sunny sky
Lingering onward dreamily
In an evening of July –

Children three that nestle near,
Eager eye and willing ear,
Pleased a simple tale to hear –

Long has paled that sunny sky:
Echoes fade and memories die:
Autumn frosts have slain July.

Still she haunts me, phantomwise,
Alice moving under skies
Never seen by waking eyes.

Children yet, the tale to hear,
Eager eye and willing ear,
Lovingly shall nestle near.

In a Wonderland they lie,
Dreaming as the days go by,
Dreaming as the summers die:

Ever drifting down the stream –
Lingering in the golden gleam –
Life, what is it but a dream?

Wynken, Blynken, and Nod
Eugene Field (1850–95)

Wynken, Blynken, and Nod one night
Sailed off in a wooden shoe, –
Sailed on a river of crystal light
Into a sea of dew.
"Where are you going, and what do you wish?"
The old moon asked the three.
"We have come to fish for the herring-fish
That live in this beautiful sea;
Nets of silver and gold have we,"
    Said Wynken,
    Blynken,
    And Nod.

The old moon laughed and sang a song,
  As they rocked in the wooden shoe;
And the wind that sped them all night long
  Ruffled the waves of dew;
The little stars were the herring-fish
  That lived in the beautiful sea.
"Now cast your nets wherever you wish, –
  Never afraid are we!"
So cried the stars to the fishermen three,
    Wynken,
    Blynken,
    And Nod.

All night long their nets they threw
  To the stars in the twinkling foam, –
Then down from the skies came the wooden shoe,
  Bringing the fishermen home:
'Twas all so pretty a sail, it seemed
  As if it could not be;
And some folk thought 'twas a dream they'd dreamed
  Of sailing that beautiful sea;
  But I shall name you the fishermen three:
      Wynken,
      Blynken,
      And Nod.

Wynken and Blynken are two little eyes,
  And Nod is a little head,
And the wooden shoe that sailed the skies
  Is a wee one's trundle-bed;
So shut your eyes while Mother sings
  Of wonderful sights that be,
And you shall see the beautiful things
  As you rock in the misty sea
  Where the old shoe rocked the fishermen three: –
      Wynken,
      Blynken,
      And Nod.

The Land of Counterpane
Robert Louis Stevenson (1850–94)

When I was sick and lay a-bed,
I had two pillows at my head,
And all my toys beside me lay
To keep me happy all the day.

And sometimes for an hour or so
I watched my leaden soldiers go,
With different uniforms and drills,
Among the bed-clothes, through the hills;

And sometimes sent my ships in fleets
All up and down among the sheets;
Or brought my trees and houses out,
And planted cities all about.

I was the giant great and still
That sits upon the pillow-hill,
And sees before him, dale and plain,
The pleasant land of counterpane.

Bed in Summer
Robert Louis Stevenson (1850–94)

In Winter I get up at night
And dress by yellow candle light.
In Summer, quite the other way,
I have to go to bed by day.

I have to go to bed and see
The birds still hopping on the tree,
Or hear the grown-up people's feet
Still going past me in the street.

And does it not seem hard to you,
When all the sky is clear and blue,
And I should like so much to play,
To have to go to bed by day?

The Star

Jane Taylor (1783–1824)

Twinkle, twinkle, little star,
How I wonder what you are!
Up above the world so high,
Like a diamond in the sky.

When the blazing sun is gone,
When he nothing shines upon,
Then you show your little light,
Twinkle, twinkle, all the night.

Then the traveller in the dark,
Thanks you for your tiny spark,
He could not see which way to go,
If you did not twinkle so.

In the dark blue sky you keep,
And often through my curtains peep,
For you never shut you eye,
Till the sun is in the sky.

As your bright and tiny spark,
Lights the traveller in the dark –
Though I know not what you are,
Twinkle, twinkle, little star.

The Land of Nod
Robert Louis Stevenson (1850–94)

From breakfast on through all the day
At home among my friends I stay,
But every night I go abroad
Afar into the land of Nod.

All by myself I have to go,
With none to tell me what to do –
All alone beside the streams
And up the mountain-sides of dreams.

The strangest things are these for me,
Both things to eat and things to see,
And many frightening sights abroad
Till morning in the land of Nod.

Try as I like to find the way,
I never can get back by day,
Nor can remember plain and clear
The curious music that I hear.

A Child's Prayer
Matilda B. Edwards (1836–1919)

God make my life a little light,
　Within the world to glow, –
A tiny flame that burneth bright,
　Wherever I may go.

God make my life a little flower,
　That giveth joy to all; –
Content to bloom in native bower
　Although its place be small.

God make my life a little song,
　That comforteth the sad;
That helpeth others to be strong,
　And makes the singer glad.

God make my life a little staff
　Whereon the weak may rest, –
That so what health and strength I have
　May serve my neighbour best.

God make my life a little hymn
　Of tenderness and praise, –
Of faith, that never waxeth dim,
　In all His wondrous ways.

Good Night and Good Morning
Richard Monckton Milnes, Lord Houghton (1809–85)

A fair little girl sat under a tree,
Sewing as long as her eyes could see;
Then smoothed her work, and folded it right,
And said, "Dear work, good night! good night!"

Such a number of rooks came over her head,
Crying, "Caw! Caw!" on their way to bed;
She said, as she watched their curious flight,
"Little black things, good night! good night!"

The horses neighed, and the oxen lowed,
The sheep's "Bleat! bleat!" came over the road;
All seeming to say, with a quiet delight,
"Good little girl, good night! good night!"

She did not say to the sun, "Good night!"
Though she saw him there like a ball of light,
For she knew he had God's time to keep
All over the world, and never could sleep.

The tall pink foxglove bowed his head,
The violets curtsied and went to bed;
And good little Lucy tied up her hair,
And said on her knees her favourite prayer.

And while on her pillow she softly lay,
She knew nothing more till again it was day;
And all things said to the beautiful sun,
"Good morning! good morning! our work is begun!"

Young Night-Thought
Robert Louis Stevenson (1850–94)

All night long and every night,
When my mama puts out the light,
I see the people marching by,
As plain as day before my eye.

Armies and emperor and kings,
All carrying different kinds of things,
And marching in so grand a way,
You never saw the like by day.

So fine a show was never seen
At the great circus on the green;
For every kind of beast and man
Is marching in that caravan.

As first they move a little slow,
But still the faster on they go,
And still beside me close I keep
Until we reach the town of Sleep.

The Sandman
Margaret Thomson Janvier (1844–1913)

The rosy clouds float overhead,

The sun is going down;

And now the sandman's gentle tread

Comes stealing through the town.

"White sand, white sand," he softly cries,

And as he shakes his hand,

Straightway there lies on babies' eyes

His gift of shining sand.

Blue eyes, grey eyes, black eyes, and brown,

As shuts the rose, they softly close, when he goes through the town.

From sunny beaches far away –

Yes, in another land –

He gathers up at break of day

His stone of shining sand.

No tempests beat that shore remote,

No ships may sail that way;

His little boat alone may float

Within that lovely bay.

Blue eyes, grey eyes, black eyes, and brown,

As shuts the rose, they softly close, when he goes through the town.

He smiles to see the eyelids close

Above the happy eyes;

And every child right well he knows, –

Oh, he is very wise!

But if, as he goes through the land,

A naughty baby cries,

His other hand takes dull grey sand

To close the wakeful eyes.

Blue eyes, grey eyes, black eyes, and brown,

As shuts the rose, they softly close, when he goes through the town.

So when you hear the sandman's song

Sound through the twilight sweet,

Be sure you do not keep him long

A-waiting in the street.

Lie softly down, dear little head,

Rest quiet, busy hands,

Till, by your bed his good-night said,

He strews the shining sands.

Blue eyes, grey eyes, black eyes, and brown,

As shuts the rose, they softly close, when he goes through the town.

Lullaby of an Infant Chief
Sir Walter Scott (1771–1832)

O, hush thee, my babie, thy sire was a knight,
Thy mother a lady, both lovely and bright;
The woods and the glens, from the towers which we see,
They are all belonging, dear babie, to thee.
O ho ro, i ri ri, cadul gu lo.

O, fear not the bugle, though loudly it blows,
It calls but the warders that guard thy repose;
Their bows would be bended, their blades would be red,
Ere the step of a foeman draws near to thy bed.
O ho ro, i ri ri, cadul gu lo.

O, hush thee, my babie, the time soon will come,
When thy sleep shall be broken by trumpet and drum;
Then hush thee, my darling, take rest while you may,
For strife comes with manhood, and waking with day.
O ho ro, i ri ri, cadul gu lo.

Wee Willie Winkie
William Miller (1810–72)

Wee Willie Winkie runs through the town,
Up stairs and down stairs in his night-gown,
Tapping at the window, crying at the lock,
Are the children in their bed, for it's past ten o'clock?

Hey, Willie Winkie, are you coming in?
The cat is singing purring sounds to the sleeping hen,
The dog's spread out on the floor, and doesn't give a cheep,
But here's a wakeful little boy who will not fall asleep!

Anything but sleep, you rogue! glowering like the moon,'
Rattling in an iron jug with an iron spoon,
Rumbling, tumbling round about, crowing like a cock,
Shrieking like I don't know what, waking sleeping folk.

Hey, Willie Winkie – the child's in a creel!
Wriggling from everyone's knee like an eel,
Tugging at the cat's ear, and confusing all her thrums
Hey, Willie Winkie – see, there he comes!"

Weary is the mother who has a dusty child,
A small short little child, who can't run on his own,
Who always has a battle with sleep before he'll close an eye
But a kiss from his rosy lips gives strength anew to me.

Poems of the
Natural World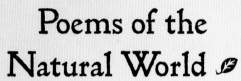

The Moon
Robert Louis Stevenson (1850–94)

The moon has a face like the clock in the hall;
She shines on thieves on the garden wall,
On streets and fields and harbour quays,
And birdies asleep in the forks of the trees.

The squalling cat and the squeaking mouse,
The howling dog by the door of the house,
The bat that lies in bed at noon,
All love to be out by the light of the moon.

But all of the things that belong to the day
Cuddle to sleep to be out of her way;
And flowers and children close their eyes
Till up in the morning the sun shall arise.

November
Alice Cary (1820–71)

The leaves are fading and falling;
The winds are rough and wild;
The birds have ceased their calling –
But let me tell you, my child,

Though day by day, as it closes,
Doth darker and colder grow,
The roots of the bright red roses
Will keep alive in the snow.

And when the winter is over,
The boughs will get new leaves,
The quail come back to the clover,
And the swallow back to the eaves.

The robin will wear on his bosom
A vest that is bright and new,
And the loveliest wayside blossom
Will shine with the sun and dew.

The leaves today are whirling;
The brooks are all dry and dumb –
But let me tell you, my darling,
The spring will be sure to come.

There must be rough, cold weather,
And winds and rains so wild;
Not all good things together
Come to us here, my child.

So, when some dear joy loses
Its beauteous summer glow,
Think how the roots of the roses
Are kept alive in the snow.

In July

Evaleen Stein (1863 – 1923)

Let us find a shady wady
Pretty little brook;
Let us have some candy handy,
And a picture book.

There all day we'll stay and play and
Never mind the heat,
While the water gleaming, streaming,
Ripples round our feet.

And we'll gather curly pearly
Mussel shells while bright
Frightened minnows darting, parting,
Scurry out of sight.

What if, what if,- heigho! my oh! –
All the "ifs" were true,
And the little fishes wishes,
Now, what would you do?

The Voice of Spring
Mary Howitt (1799–1888)

The Voice of Spring
I am coming, I am coming!
Hark! the little bee is humming;
See, the lark is soaring high
In the blue and sunny sky;
And the gnats are on the wing,
Wheeling round in airy ring.

See, the yellow catkins cover
All the slender willows over!
And on the banks of mossy green
Starlike primroses are seen;
And, their clustering leaves below,
White and purple violets blow.

Hark! the new-born lambs are bleating,
And the cawing rooks are meeting
In the elms, – a noisy crowd;
All the birds are singing loud;
And the first white butterfly
In the sunshine dances by.

Look around thee, look around!
Flowers in all the fields abound;
Every running stream is bright;
All the orchard trees are white;
And each small and waving shoot
Promises sweet flowers and fruit.

Turn thine eyes to earth and heaven:
God for thee the spring has given,
Taught the birds their melodies,
Clothed the earth, and cleared the skies,
For thy pleasure or thy food:
Pour thy soul in gratitude.

Birds in Summer (extract)
Mary Howitt (1799–1888)

How pleasant the life of a bird must be,
Flitting about in each leafy tree;
In the leafy trees so broad and tall,
Like a green and beautiful palace hall,
With its airy chambers light and boon,
That open to sun and stars and moon;
That open to the bright blue sky,
And the frolicsome winds as they wander by.

They have left their nests on the forest bough;
Those homes of delight they need not now;
And the young and the old they wander out,
And traverse their green world round about;
And hark! at the top of this leafy hall,
How one to the other in love they call!
"Come up! Come up!" they seem to say,
"Where the topmost twigs in the breezes sway."

"Come up! come up! for the world is fair
Where the merry leaves dance in the summer air."
And the birds below give back the cry,
"We come, we come to the branches high."
How pleasant the lives of the birds must be,
Living in love in a leafy tree!
And away through the air what joy to go,
And to look on the green, bright earth below!

How pleasant the life of a bird must be,

Skimming about on the breezy sea,

Cresting the billows like silvery foam,

Then wheeling away to its cliff-built home!

What joy it must be to sail, upborne,

By a strong free wing, through the rosy morn,

To meet the young sun, face to face,

And pierce, like a shaft, the boundless space!

To pass through the bowers of the silver cloud;

To sing in the thunder hall aloud;

To spread out the wings for a wild, free flight

With the upper cloud-wings, oh, what delight!

Oh, what would I give, like a bird, to go,

Right on through the arch of the sun lit bow,

And see how the waterdrops are kissed

Into green and yellow and amethyst.

The Rainbow

Christina Rossetti (1830–94)

Boats sail on the rivers,
And ships sail on the seas;
But clouds that sail across the sky
Are prettier than these.

There are bridges on the rivers,
As pretty as you please;
But the bow that bridges heaven,
And overtops the trees,
And builds a road from earth to sky,
Is prettier far than these.

Jack Frost
Gabriel Setoun (1861 – 1930)

The door was shut, as doors should be,
　Before you went to bed last night;
Yet Jack Frost has got in, you see,
　And left your window silver white.

He must have waited till you slept;
　And not a single word he spoke,
But pencilled o'er the panes and crept
　Away again before you woke.

And now you cannot see the hills
　Nor fields that stretch beyond the lane;
But there are fairer things than these
　His fingers traced on every pane.

Rocks and castles towering high;
　Hills and dales, and streams and fields;
And knights in armor riding by,
　With nodding plumes and shining shields.

And here are little boats, and there
　Big ships with sails spread to the breeze;
And yonder, palm trees waving fair
　On islands set in silver seas,

And butterflies with gauzy wings;
  And herds of cows and flocks of sheep;
And fruit and flowers and all the things
  You see when you are sound asleep.

For, creeping softly underneath
  The door when all the lights are out,
Jack Frost takes every breath you breathe,
  And knows the things you think about.

He paints them on the window-pane
  In fairy lines with frozen steam;
And when you wake you see again
  The lovely things you saw in dream.

At the Seaside
Robert Louis Stevenson (1850–94)

When I was down beside the sea
A wooden spade they gave to me
To dig the sandy shore.
My holes were empty like a cup,
In every hole the sea came up,
Till it could come no more.

The Wind and the Moon (extract)
George Macdonald (1824–1905)

Said the Wind to the Moon, "I will blow you out;
You stare
In the air
Like a ghost in a chair,
Always looking what I am about –
I hate to be watched; I'll blow you out."

The Wind blew hard, and out went the Moon.
So, deep
On a heap
Of clouds to sleep,
Down lay the Wind, and slumbered soon,
Muttering low, "I've done for that Moon."

He turned in his bed; she was there again!
On high
In the sky,
With her one ghost eye,
The Moon shone white and alive and plain.
Said the Wind, "I will blow you out again."

The Wind blew hard, and the Moon grew dim.
"With my sledge,
And my wedge,
I have knocked off her edge!
If only I blow right fierce and grim,
The creature will soon be dimmer than dim."

He blew and he blew, and she thinned to a thread.
"One puff
More's enough
To blow her to snuff!
One good puff more where the last was bred,
And glimmer, glimmer, glum will go the thread."

He blew a great blast, and the thread was gone.
In the air
Nowhere
Was a moonbeam bare;
Far off and harmless the shy stars shone –
Sure and certain the Moon was gone!

Spring
William Blake (1757–1827)

Sound the flute!
Now it's mute!
Bird's delight,
Day and night,
Nightingale,
In the dale,
Lark in sky, –
Merrily,
Merrily merrily, to welcome in the year.

Little boy,
Full of joy;
Little girl,
Sweet and small;
Cock does crow,
So do you;
Merry voice,
Infant noise;
Merrily, merrily, to welcome in the year.

Little lamb,

Here I am;

Come and lick

My white neck;

Let me pull

Your soft wool;

Let me kiss

Your soft face;

Merrily, merrily, to welcome in the year.

The Snowbird's Song
Francis C. Woodworth (1812–59)

The ground was all covered with snow one day,
And two little sisters were busy at play,
When a snowbird was sitting close by on a tree,
And merrily singing his chick-a-de-dee,

>Chick-a-de-dee, chick-a-de-dee,

And merrily singing his chick-a-de-dee.
He had not been singing that tune very long,
Ere Emily heard him, so loud was his song:
"Oh, sister, look out of the window," said she;
"Here's a dear little bird singing chick-a-de-dee.

>Chick-a-de-dee, chick-a-de-dee,

"Oh, mother, do get him some stockings and shoes,
And a nice little frock, and a hat if he choose;
I wish he'd come into the parlor and see
How warm we would make him, poor chick-a-de-dee."

>Chick-a-de-dee, chick-a-de-dee,

"There is one, my dear child, though I cannot tell who,
Has clothed me already, and warm enough too.
Good morning! Oh, who are so happy as we?"
And away he went singing his chick-a-de-dee.

>Chick-a-de-dee, chick-a-de-dee.

April! April! Are You Here?
Dora Read Goodale (1866–1915)

April! April! are you here?
Oh, how fresh the wind is blowing!
See! the sky is bright and clear,
Oh, how green the grass is growing!
April! April! are you here?

April! April! is it you?
See how fair the flowers are springing!
Sun is warm and brooks are clear,
Oh, how glad the birds are singing!
April! April! is it you?

April! April! you are here!
Though your smiling turn to weeping,
Though your skies grow cold and drear,
Though your gentle winds are sleeping,
April! April! you are here!

The Echoing Green
William Blake (1757–1827)

The sun does arise,
And make happy the skies;
The merry bells ring
To welcome the spring;
The skylark and thrush,
The birds of the bush,
Sing louder around
To the bell's cheerful sound,
While our sports shall be seen
On the Echoing Green.

Old John with white hair,
Does laugh away care,
Sitting under the oak,
Among the old folk.
They laugh at our play,
And soon they all say:
'Such, such were the joys
When we all, girls and boys,
In our youth time were seen
On the Echoing Green.'

Till the little ones, weary,

No more can be merry;

The sun does descend,

And our sports have an end.

Round the laps of their mothers

Many sisters and brother,

Like birds in their nest,

Are ready for rest,

And sport no more seen

On the darkening Green.

Picture Credits

1 Emile Vernon (1872-1919) *The Three Graces* © Christie's Images Ltd - ARTOTHEK

3 Walter Firle (1859-1929) *A Good Book* © Christie's Images Ltd./SuperStock

4 Elisabeth Louise Vigee Le Brun (1755-1842) *Madame Vigee-lebrun And Her Daughter* © SuperStock/SuperStock

7 Frederick Morgan (1856-1927) *Me Too?, c.1901* © Christie's Images Ltd./SuperStock

9 Luigi Toro (1836-1900) *A Faithful Friend* © Christie's Images Ltd./SuperStock

10-11 Hans Andersen Brendekilde (1857-1942) *The New Doll*, 1924 © Christie's Images Ltd - ARTOTHEK

13 John George Brown (1831-1913) *Young Girl in a New York Garden*, 1871 © Christie's Images Ltd - ARTOTHEK

15 Paul Wagner (1852-1937) *Am Steg*, 1889 © ARTOTHEK

18 George Sheridan Knowles, (1863-1931) *There They Go*, 1901 © SuperStock/SuperStock

22-23 Frants Henningsen (1850-1908) *Children Of the Photographer Tillges*, 1884 © Christie's Images Ltd./SuperStock

25 John George Brown (1831-1913) *The Picnic*, 1861 © Christie's Images Ltd./SuperStock

27 Claude Monet (1840-1926) *Luncheon*, 1868 © U. Edelman-Stadel Museum-ARTOTHEK

31 Arthur Percy Dixon (*fl.*1884-1917) *The Princess and The Frog* © Christie's Images Ltd-ARTOTHEK

32 Robert Cree Crawford (1842-1924) *My Best Friend* © Christie's Images Ltd./SuperStock

35 Frederic Leighton (1830-96) *Gulnihal*, 1886 © Christie's Images Ltd-ARTOTHEK

37 Ramsay Richard Reinagle, R.A. (1775-1862*) A Group Portrait of Robert, James and Mary Sarah*, 1831 © Christie's Images Ltd./SuperStock

38 William-Adolphe Bouguereau (1825-1905) *Little Girl*, 1878 © Fine Art Images/SuperStock

42-43 Henrietta Ronner-Knip (1821-1909) *Studies of a Long-haired White Cat*, 1896 © Christie's Images Ltd-ARTOTHEK

46 Federigo Andreotti (1847-1930) *The Letter* © Christie's Images Ltd-ARTOTHEK

50-51 Walter Hunt (1861-1941) *The Foster Mother*, 1887 © Christie's Images Ltd-ARTOTHEK

53 William-Adolphe Bouguereau (1825-1905) *Child Braiding A Crown*, 1874 © Buyenlarge/SuperStock

55 Walter Hunt (1861-1941) *Motherless: The Shepherd's Pet*, 1897 © Christie's Images Ltd./SuperStock

57 George Sheridan Knowles (1863-1931), *Feeding the Pigeons* © Fine Art Photographic Library/SuperStock

58 Frederic Leighton (1830-96) *Kittens* © Christie's Images Ltd-ARTOTHEK

61 Walter Hunt (1861-1941) *Farmyard Friends*, 1923 © Christie's Images Ltd./SuperStock

63 Frederick Morgan (1856-1927) *The Garland* © Christie's Images Ltd-ARTOTHEK

Indexes